Copyright © 2024 by Walter the Educator

All rights reserved. No part of this book may be reproduced in any manner whatsoever without written permission except in the case of brief quotations embodied in critical articles and reviews.

First Printing, 2024

Disclaimer
This book is a literary work; the story is not about specific persons, locations, situations, and/or circumstances unless mentioned in a historical context. Any resemblance to real persons, locations, situations, and/or circumstances is coincidental. This book is for entertainment and informational purposes only. The author and publisher offer this information without warranties expressed or implied. No matter the grounds, neither the author nor the publisher will be accountable for any losses, injuries, or other damages caused by the reader's use of this book. The use of this book acknowledges an understanding and acceptance of this disclaimer.

Celebrating the City of Bali is a collectible souvenir book that belongs to the Celebrating Cities Book Series by Walter the Educator. Collect them all and more books at WaltertheEducator.com

Celebrating the City of Bali

Walter the Educator

Silent King Books

SILENT KING BOOKS
SKB

BALI

In the cradle of the sea's embrace,

Celebrating the City of

Bali

A gem emerges, known as Bali's place.

Celebrating the City of
Bali

Where emerald fields and sapphire tides

Celebrating the City of

Bali

Entwine beneath the heavens wide.

Celebrating the City of
Bali

Mystic rites at twilight's fall,

Celebrating the City of
Bali

In Besakih, the mother's call.

Celebrating the City of

Bali

Candles flicker in the dusk,

Celebrating the City of

Bali

Scents of incense, soft and husk.

Celebrating the City of
Bali

Sunsets paint the western sky,

Celebrating the City of

Bali

As day succumbs to night's lullaby.

Celebrating the City of
Bali

Jimbaran's shores, aglow with flame,

Celebrating the City of Bali

Where stories told and songs acclaim.

Celebrating the City of

Bali

Mount Agung, in majesty,

Celebrating the City of
Bali

Oversees this isle of harmony.

Celebrating the City of
Bali

Sacred heights and fiery core,

Celebrating the City of Bali

Silent keeper of the lore.

Celebrating the City of

Bali

Culinary arts in spices blend,

Celebrating the City of
Bali

Flavors bold that never end.

Celebrating the City of
Bali

Nasi Goreng, Sate's kiss,

Celebrating the City of
Bali

Balinese feasts of simple bliss.

Celebrating the City of

Bali

Gamelan's notes, in silken streams,

Celebrating the City of Bali

Weave the night with haunting dreams.

Celebrating the City of
Bali

Dancers move in rhythmic trance,

Captivating with each glance.

Celebrating the City of

Bali

Balinese hearts in kindness beat,

Celebrating the City of

Bali

Strangers met with smiles sweet.

Celebrating the City of
Bali

A spirit born of ancient ties,

Celebrating the City of

Bali

Of open arms and warm goodbyes.

Celebrating the City of
Bali

Bali's spirit, wild and free,

Celebrating the City of

Bali

Lives in land and air and sea.

Celebrating the City of
Bali

In every heart it finds its place,

Celebrating the City of

Bali

An endless source of gentle grace.

Celebrating the City of
Bali

Eternal Bali, ever bright,

Celebrating the City of

Bali

In morning's gold and evening's light.

Celebrating the City of
Bali

A paradise on earth's embrace,

Celebrating the City of

Bali

Where beauty dwells in every space.

Celebrating the City of
Bali

Each path, a story yet untold,

Celebrating the City of
Bali

In Bali's arms, forever hold.

Celebrating the City of Bali

An island bathed in nature's kiss,

Celebrating the City of

Bali

A timeless haven of pure bliss.

Celebrating the City of

Bali

So let us raise a song, a cheer,

Celebrating the City of

Bali

For Bali's land we hold so dear.

Celebrating the City of
Bali

In every breath, in every sigh,

Celebrating the City of

Bali

The spirit of Bali will never die.

Celebrating the City of
Bali

ABOUT THE CREATOR

Walter the Educator is one of the pseudonyms for Walter Anderson. Formally educated in Chemistry, Business, and Education, he is an educator, an author, a diverse entrepreneur, and he is the son of a disabled war veteran. "Walter the Educator" shares his time between educating and creating. He holds interests and owns several creative projects that entertain, enlighten, enhance, and educate, hoping to inspire and motivate you.

Follow, find new works, and stay up to date
with Walter the Educator™
at WaltertheEducator.com

Milton Keynes UK
Ingram Content Group UK Ltd.
UKHW050216130724
445574UK00013B/514

9 798330 267644